The Effigies

Other Books by Robert Hill Long

The Power to Die (1987)
The Work of the Bow (1997)

WEST HARTFORD, CONNECTICUT

The Effigies

Robert Hill Long

Copyright © 1998 by Robert Hill Long

All rights reserved.

Manufactured in the United States of America.
Printed on acid-free paper.

Direct all inquiries to the publisher:

PLINTH BOOKS
P.O. Box 271118
West Hartford, CT 06127-1118

FIRST EDITION

Library of Congress Card Catalog Number: 97-65103

ISBN 1-887628-04-5 (cloth)
1-887628-05-3 (paper)

Quotation after Contents page: from "The Sparrow," *Selected Poems of William Carlos Williams,* © 1969 New Directions Books

Cover photograph © 1978 by Robert Chamberlain

Cover and interior design by Charles Casey Martin

✷ Acknowledgments

The Fiction Review: "Aquarium."

Flash Fiction: Very Short Stories (W. W. Norton): "The Restraints."

Hayden's Ferry Review: "Walking Sticks."

The Kenyon Review: "Dirt Yards," "Bonemeal," "Lactarius Indigo," "Devotion," "Brick Dust," "Oranges," "A Well-Regarded Man," "Pigeons."

Massachusetts Review: "Virgin Oil," "Fleur-de-lys."

New Delta Review: "On Duty."

New England Review: "The Coral Sea," "The Past," "Angel's Trumpet," "Razors," "Yellow Stars," "Tags," "The Hammock Prayer," "Revolutions of Dust," "Underwear," "The Shape It Takes."

New Orleans Review: "In Country."

Nexus: "Parasites," "Umbrella Trees," "Lean and Fat," "Revival."

Pares cum Paribus (World Wide Web): "Ghost Powder," "Jugglers," "The Archway," "Walking Sticks."

Poetry East: "Euterpe," "Erato," "Terpsichore," "Thalia," "Melpomene," "Clio," "Polymnia," "Urania," "Calliope."

The Prose Poem: "Lucky Tobies."

The Prose Poem: An International Journal: "Hurt to See."

Quarterly West: "The Restraints," "Hermit Crab," "Lye."

Stand (UK): "Flamingo Tongue."

Virginia Quarterly Review: "Eyes of the Swordfish," "Stealing Dirt."

Warren Wilson Review: "Gamblers."

Web del Sol: World Wide Web reprints of "The Coral Sea," "The Past," "Devotion," "Melpomene," "Clio," "Calliope," "Revival," "Bonemeal," "Lucky Tobies," "The Restraints."

Thanks to the editors for printing these pieces, and for permission to reprint them. Richard Jones *(Poetry East)* and T. R. Hummer *(Kenyon Review, New England Review)* were especially supportive. The North Carolina Arts Council gave me fellowship time in which this book was conceived and begun; the National Endowment for the Arts gave me a fellowship during which it was completed. Lee Meitzen Grue put me up in New Orleans at the most crucial time. Tess Gallagher gave me a valuable reconception of the book's look and pace. And from the beginning to the end of the writing was the legendary Group 18 of Northampton, Massachusetts, with all those Monday night potlucks of home-cooked critique.

This book is for my brothers Andy and Mike, and for my sister Susan, all still in the South, where I wish I was.

❦ Contents

Revolutions of Dust   3

A Century of Southern Light

The Coral Sea 7 / The Past   8
Parasites 10 / Umbrella Trees 12 / Angel's Trumpet 13
Virgin Oil 14 / Lean and Fat 16
Underwear 17 / Aquarium 18 / The Shapes It Takes 19
Enemies 21 / Walking Sticks 23
Devotion 24 / Lye 25 / Dirt Yards 27
Pigeons 29 / Oranges 31
A Well-Regarded Man 33 / Two Toyshops 35

The Streets of the Muses

Euterpe 39 / Terpsichore 40
Thalia 41 / Polymnia 42 / Urania 44
Erato 46 / Melpomene 47 / Clio 49 / Calliope 51

Toward a Bad End

Revival 55 / Bonemeal 57 / Eyes of the Swordfish 59
Tags 61 / Flamingo Tongue 63 / Hermit Crab 65
Lucky Tobies 67 / Gamblers 68 / On Duty 70
Hurt to See 72 / Razors 73 / Stealing Dirt 75
Fleur-de-lys 77 / Lactarius Indigo 79 / The Restraints 80
In Country 82 / Brick Dust 84
Ghost Powder 86 / The Hammock Prayer 88
The Archway 90 / Yellow Stars 92

The Author   95

A Note to the Reader

The Effigies is an elegiac sequence, set in a Deep South riverport. Its chronology tends toward the last fifty years, but often goes much further back, since this book is as much about cultural history as about minor, personal histories. Each piece is a self-contained narrative, but its characters, families, streets, neighborhoods, and incidents, however isolated from each other, belong to a common climate and history: the book's city. *The Effigies* attempts not to comprehend but rather apprehend that city.

a wisp of feathers
flattened to the pavement,
wings spread symmetrically
as if in flight,
the head gone,
the black escutcheon of the breast
indecipherable,
an effigy of a sparrow,
a dried wafer only,
left to say
and it says it
without offense,
beautifully;
this was I,
a sparrow.
I did my best;
farewell.

—William Carlos Williams

The Effigies

REVOLUTIONS OF DUST

This was the house his grandfather's great-grandfather raised: native cypress shingle, heart pine panelling, hand-carved cherry banisters, outside the old city wall, on the avenue called Elysian Fields. The house that was passed down to him. Yesterday title passed to bankers: their bulldozers are already parked outside.

He lies on the floor of his grandmother's bedroom. What's left? army surplus sleeping bag, a copy of Donne's final sermons. A blank book he could fill with testimony about what fifteen years of failures have failed to teach him. His left hand is wrapped in a t-shirt bloody from punching his way in through a back window. It's the end of his last night here.

In dawn light he reads aloud from Donne. "Every puff of wind within these walls may blow the father into the son's eyes. Where is the body? And what should an eye do where there is nothing to be seen?" He aims the words where the portraits hung: two spots darker, cleaner than the wall chipped and faded around them. "The skin, the body are ground away, trod away; they are destroyed. Who knows the revolutions of dust?"

The blank squares of his grandfather, his grandmother. They left a century of morocco-bound books and velvet furniture to secure his future—which he sold off years ago. He puts his face to the floor to smell the dust: old skin, grandmother hair ground to a white powder. He himself feels like an empty tent of skin. Who he was is gone, broken down into children he passes playing in the gutter, into winos picking through church dustbins.

The gash in his hand still oozes. He'll have to find a doctor who will accept a few quotes from Donne instead of cash. Across the city, the third bell of the day; through the broken window, the cry of a neighbor-baby. Both say God is breaking down, down into small, distant sounds. And the Bible says take up your burden, walk. Walk through this city built the depth of a grave below sea level. Wherever he walks, he'll walk in the ghost of water.

Hungry among the bench-huggers he'll keep moving, among the ones who implore Jesus in the middle of taxi-crazed intersections. His hair will start leaving him, then his voice; he'll gain a limp, an ugly cough. And maybe begin to lose the shame of debts older than he can remember. This was the house. And this, inching through the window, is the first light of dispossession. In an hour the sheriff will get up, come hunting for him along all the side streets of the Elysian Fields.

A Century of Southern Light

THE CORAL SEA

A cardinal flies out a broken warehouse window, startling the white-haired housecleaner on the corner. The red wings light a place in memory as she waits for the Desire bus. Cotton bales used to pile up on this building's noisy loading dock. Across the boulevard, she hauled braids of garlic and blond-leafed bundles of sugarcane from her daddy's flatbed truck to a stall in the farm market's breezeway. She'd pause for breath, brush city fog out of her face, and watch young men wrestle the cotton into a wall, ready to ship. The black gleam of their arms and backs vanished behind the wall, but not their laughter.

Between a depression and a war, the city offered itself to her in the shouts of flower vendors. Lint-headed boys danced past her, dangling plucked chickens on colored string. She let the city take her in. The shuttered doors of good houses opened into a wealth of heirlooms that she polished and dusted as though they were her own: armoires, cases of heavy silverware, lacy ivory statuettes. Each evening sailors strolled out of barracks by the embarkation depot. First white, then black sailors, all in uniforms white as her own. She'd sit on her stoop fanning her arms and neck, hearing their laughter fan out among side streets that held no more love or danger then than today, when the bus is unusually late.

She crosses her ankles, inspects each white shoe for smudges. That cardinal must be nesting in the warehouse. She peered through a window last year and saw nothing—long shafts of light, full of eddying cotton dust. She still has a letter—pushed to the back of her underwear drawer—from one of those sailors, another farm kid the city took in. He wrote about apples, how many it took to make pies enough for fifty navy pilots in 1942. The letter's postmarked a week before her twentieth birthday: the day his carrier began steaming toward a rendezvous whose name—along with a few other harmless words—would be blacked out by an overworked censor.

THE PAST

Greened-over statues hold the city down like paperweights placed on an old treaty. When these effigies were men, their warm hands held maps of the New World flat so the emperor could see all he was signing away. One or two names drying on the parchment might end up in bronze; two centuries past, they were functionaries who shook hands as required, disdaining each other's language.

Some statues survive as local jokes: Silent George pointing to the river, condom on his finger, crumpled beer can in hand. An orator for the defeated rebels, his nameplate lies under some teenage boy's car seat, if it wasn't already tossed off a wharf on a dare one Saturday night.

Each year the cemetery paths get a fresh load of bleached oyster shells, but the open butcher stalls—marble slabs haloed by blackflies—are gone. So, too, the factory specializing in child-sized caskets. The Victorian fashion of bedding the corpse among orchids and plumage almost killed off the snowy egrets. Carts piled with dead birds stopped at the mortician's en route to the milliner's, where the rest of the feathers were plucked for ladies' wedding and funeral hats.

But fashion can be defeated, like yellow fever, like the river at flood stage. Above the cash register of the oldest bar in town, there's a photo of a shotgun house half submerged in sun-flattened water. A flatboat's moored to a side stairway; the stairs lead up to a woman. Her embroidered tablecloths and antimacassars drifted out to the Gulf a century ago, but she abides in Sunday whites and feathered hat, resolutely ignoring the bartender and drinkers nursing their rum and colas. For her only the future appeared barbarous.

The slave market, a few blocks past the bar, is preserved not because of the chic boutiques that inhabit its shell, but for a cornice of marble ram-skulls found nowhere else in the South. A block beyond that, a gang of boys light cigarettes and compare knives in a rusted-out sedan on concrete blocks. If it had wheels, they'd all be gone north.

PARASITES

The lacy ferns that fetch the highest greenhouse prices grow rank and out of reach downtown, in cracked stone columns and eaves of buildings like this museum—a survivor of three colonial languages. On the steps, a boy peels last week's sunburn from his arms, flings dead skin to the plaza pigeons. Inside, his parents take a quick bored tour of relics—cutlasses, candle molds, leg irons, wax figures in period costume.

When the overcast morning lightens, the shouts of mule-drivers carry farther, echo in the museum arcade where two cannons aim across the river they were meant to guard forever. Touring schoolchildren reach into the cannon mouths to touch the moldy cork, then pull back laughing. Their fingers are blackish-green with what the teacher calls "living history."

Across the square, a wife nags her husband to have his portrait done in pastel or watercolor, so she can carry a bit of the city's color to their drab, weedy parish. The artist's fence-hung gallery features celebrities copied from magazine poses. At the wife's feet, pigeons stab at crumbs falling from the half-eaten biscuit she waves to support her argument. At last the husband consents to be pictured, but only in charcoal.

The afternoon continues to lighten. On the museum's facade, blackened plaster and exposed brick affirm their kinship to the river silt and clay from which they were reared. The head curator—bald, anemic, a history buff—complains to everyone who visits his austere office that the ferns are parasites: they break down the mortar, they weaken the structure. The roof's too slippery to reach them with herbicides; he proposes exterminating the pigeons instead. But the rest of the day eases past with no lasting decision reached.

At dusk, a wino steps out from the darkening arcade and unslings his broken-necked guitar. His voice wobbles and cracks; his torn, rope-belted pants drive the last sightseers off the steps and benches. Behind him, the Confederate submarine is slightly more oxidized from all the small moist hands laid against it. The pigeons have picked the plaza clean, they clatter up among the ferns to roost. Outside history, in ordinary darkness, they nod, puff out iridescent ruffs, sleep.

UMBRELLA TREES

It's not long till morning. Two balding men in wine-spotted tuxedo shirts keep the empty hotel ballroom fully lit to argue the fine points of cigar ash, the sugar content of cognacs. A hundred miles south, a line of hungry white pelicans glides between rose-tipped Gulf swells. A cemetery mule shakes dew off its ears, gives its tether a healthy jerk, pushes its head between headstones to crop the grass. In the cathedral, mice sniff around the communion rail, then retire as usual to the choir-robe closet.

Streetlights dim. Night-shift taxis switch off fog lights, bang manhole covers all the way back to the garage. The boulevards of wide homes and colonial oaks give off a humid odor of sleep long after dawn. On other streets—pinched, potholed, jammed with shotgun houses and the barking of strays—the only silence left is the silence of umbrella trees: their torch-white blossoms held straight up, still tightly furled.

A man under the train bridge, wrapped in last Sunday's paper, may bite the inside of his lip as the aroma of coffee and home fries drifts over the levee. But it's the image of a woman laughing into a pillow that fills his mouth with spit. He watches a tug wallow upstream, a shirtless boy whistling and pissing off its stern. He'd like to piss a healthy clear arc like he used to, champagne-drunk on a twelfth-floor balcony, hearing it hit the river with a faint fizz while his wife—naked except for his boiled shirt-front and cummerbund—snored on the floor.

Seven a.m. The buggy-driver pushes a new plastic geranium through the peak of his mule's straw hat, adjusts her blinders before harnessing the tourist buggy. In the flower-bed off the main square, a city laborer kneels, singing loudly in Spanish as he uproots dead annuals. River-mist is already smoking off the fronds of palms, off the monsignor's wide sailcloth parasol.

ANGEL'S TRUMPET

To understand the angel's trumpet, look into its creamy mouth at the sexual organ. Powdered with a confectioners' sugar of pollen, it will perform its one task at the first clap of summer thunder. In this plant, rank and brilliant, the jungle may resume dominion over the city's shabby outskirts where country people show up like flotsam.

Today, it's enough that the rains of late May sweep this flowering dirt-yard. The quiet rains carry flecks of paint and torn paper through a hole in the half-collapsed back porch; they carry off the light dry husks of ants, earthworms, failed baby birds. Behind the house and the angel's trumpet, the ditch shines with running water. Everything taken away here enriches some other place of mud snails and egrets, it's the law of the delta.

In the kitchen a woman tugs at her housedress, yawns. She's not too old to travel, but will never see any more of the mountains than the color photo of the Rockies pasted up by the stove. She tore it from a travel magazine delivered to her years ago by mistake. Once nuns taught her to repeat *Levavi oculos meos in montes.* While lifting this mountain out of its binding she felt a strange shame—the kind she might feel if caught peeping through a rich woman's picture window.

Today it's enough to step out, during a lull in the rains, onto the porch she'll never fix. In one wide look she takes in the snow-colored clouds building over the river. Then she steps into the muddy yard to fill a glass bowl with the white silence of angel's trumpets. Compared to these blossoms the glossy, pasted-up mountain suffers—what with mildew, grease stains from the stove, the acids embedded in the image that are eating it inside out.

VIRGIN OIL

In the old quarter there are black benches, a few, where a tainted French survives in women who softly tear baguettes for pigeons. Their conversations might yield nothing but bunions, progress of a lace embroidery, the ill-advised repainting of a certain drugstore. The speech itself is a vat of virgin olive oil into which a tin of molasses has leaked, drop by drop. Around them the other, the southern talk crackles like bacon, spills its grit and grease to the pavement. Tourist cameras snip out a few square feet of the old women's quarter, flatten it, silence it so that it can be flown a thousand miles north and end up in a shoe box full of souvenir menus and matchbooks.

Unperturbed, the woman in the white mushroom hat draws the long loaf from her Woolworth's bag. She breaks it into eight equal sections while she chats to herself about black clothes. When her father died, black was all her mother was allowed. When her own husband died, she found it acceptable to limit her display to a black coat and shoes, some days merely black kid gloves. Every day in the plaza she sees young women dress wholly in black: their skirts, their scarves and stockings have nothing to do with death or grief or even memory. Most are too young to remember anything but the first plum-colored spots in their underpants. The language they use is full of smoke, it sounds giddy, shamelessly drunk.

Dozens of hollowed-out crusts gather at her milk-colored flats. Pigeons are smart, she remarks: they don't waste time on the hard as long as they can have the soft. Already they strut toward another bench where one of her third cousins prepares to baby them with day-old croissants, with soft gutturals, kissing noises. Whisking crumbs off her skirt, she rises, chooses a narrow alley to avoid the Japanese and German cameras. Time to make her daily stop at the peach-colored church behind her house.

It takes two breaths to push the heavy door open. Before closing it, she allows the organist's Gregorian monody to sink into the cooling paving bricks behind her. One knee to the floor, then she goes to pester the priest to stop studying about teen pregnancy counseling; she leads him to the massive Douay Bible with gold-trimmed pages. In the dry gray light of the sanctuary, the book spills over his lap: *Je suis le pain de vie, le pain du ciel.* She rubs one eye, then the other, taking in his baritone full of the bread, the wine she'll drink nowhere else in this life.

LEAN AND FAT

Raking coppery magnolia leaves, the park gardener traps a bunch between one hand and the bamboo teeth, transferring them to a square of canvas. Eighty years ago, durable cloth could be a man's greatest asset: the jacket that repelled malarial mosquitoes, or those striped awnings bearing the shopkeeper's red initial, which kept the sun off his soft Caribbean fruit. The small statue of Jesus beneath myrtle trees speaks of centuries when women and men endured lean and fat years alike in a single unceremonious robe.

From his bench, an old man examines Christ's granite drapery: pitted, fogged with lichen. His own leisure suit gets baggier by the year on his shrinking frame; he can't help wondering what to do with the closetful of suits grown too big to wear. The statue's hand gestures toward the always-poor—two sleep nearby in the monkey-grass, bare toes sticking up. The gardener's shiny trouser-knees say, Hang on to what you've still got.

But the myrtle bark—smooth, pale in the weak sun—shames him. It's like looking down at his own ankles, polished bald by a life of black banker's socks, as he bears down on the bathroom scales each Sunday morning. Where did his male weight go? All these years, where did they come to him from? He doesn't care for the prospect of confinement in pajamas when his sons, wearing his retailored suits, bring sweets to the nursing home.

But now the gardener tells him to lift his feet—he needs to get at some renegade leaves—and atop the myrtle a mockingbird starts up, at full volume, variations on the song that ten thousand years have scarcely altered.

UNDERWEAR

The subway orator, how will he prevail with nothing underfoot but mud and fossils? A handswidth of sun feeble on his vinyl satchel, he stoops: a lost wedding ring may swim up to him. How to locate a corner where he can lecture, can preach and recite without losing his voice to the wind?

Behind him a police corporal putters along on a scooter. He notes the man's baldness, fur hat in one hand, the satchel with its Trailways sticker. The day is too mild for him to harass the old bum. He parks the scooter by the playground swings and begins picking up a litter of ice cream sticks, gum wrappers. One street over a boom box shouts, "More music, less talk!" When the wind lifts, shredded plastic bags tremble in the catalpa tree.

Two stocky women, between them a duffel bag stuffed with dirty clothes, cross the square. Busy keeping their mouths shut about this stranger who rubs his bald black skull to a shine with a scrap of fur, they miss the bit of underwear that slips free. Floating briefly, it settles to the pavement. The orator yawns a bass, gigantic, drawn-out O that hurries the women away toward the laundromat.

Inside the fur hat's lining he can feel twenty-five, thirty quarters, a few bills. He'll open today's mission with the need for a personal savior, and finish with vodka and Tabasco-scrambled eggs. If there's no place to sleep then, he'll hit the one street where sightseers waste vacation cash all night. There he can preach charity and home.

Across the square, inmates of a mental home have been led out for a walk. Attached to each other by the fingers, soiled sleeves, coattails, they balance toward a patch of sunlit flagstone where the wisp of forgotten underwear—it must be a girl's—trembles a little. A stray gust and it jumps suddenly past the bench where the orator polishes his head, into the low rattling branches of the catalpa: shivering, starved, the flickering sex of something worn once and lost.

AQUARIUM

Into a dozen half-empty ketchup bottles the barmaid funnels a big can of ketchup. Screwing on the caps she remarks "That's that," wipes her hands on a reddened rag. On the window-ledge above her head stands a clarinet, mouth down, its split reed held together with a band-aid. In the kitchen the cooks finish up, drain off the hot deep-fry fat flecked with fish batter. The bar-room is the indistinct gray-green of jungle before rain. Atmosphere presses down against the adjoining patio with its banana plants and tin roof, against the windows that admit humid gray river-light.

At the far end of the all but empty bar an aquarium flashes with moonfish and neon gobies. There, a young couple—they've paid up—coax their infant girl to feel the mossy water. "Go on, baby doll," the mother laughs. The father lifts the girl's chubby arm with his right hand, using his left to force her fingers into the water. The little girl makes a noise that might be delight, fascination, outrage. It snaps the slow circular rhythm of the fish, scatters them like broken glass toward the bottom.

The peace of Sunday afternoons is so fragile. The barmaid, wiping ashtrays, stares at the backs of the couple's heads as if that might force them to apologize and leave—then decides to use a blues tape turned up loud. In the exposed beams above the bar a chameleon has caught a moth: it bites the thorax so that wings flutter outside its mouth, like paper fans old people use in airless churches along the levee.

Rain, gathering weight over the river, bursts against the tin roof, streams down windows patterned like the scales of a carp. "We'll have to run for it now," the man complains. Neither he nor his wife moves. The baby shakes her wet fist in their faces. The ceiling fan continues to revolve in dozens of up-ended, polished pint glasses. The chameleon, letting the two severed wings fall like faded ginkgo leaves, slowly—from head to tail—turns green.

THE SHAPES IT TAKES

Two great hands God gave the guitar player. The wooden leg was added later to explain the difference between music and greed; the windbreaker, ripped at the back, means No place left to go but forward. Seated on his milk-crate on Royal Street, he can squint at the strings between songs and see the six- and twelve-string rows of power lines that ran alongside the bus to Memphis, Chicago, Detroit.

His uncle conducted the band—boys with dented pawnshop instruments—with a drumstick wrapped in duct tape and aluminum foil to give off a shine. Four and five nights a week: roadhouses, barbecue joints, once in a while a ballroom. Amazed and frightened by the cash counted into his hand each night, he kept the thin layer of fifties beneath the arch support of his right shoe.

The parable about greed caught him after a job in Cleveland. The rest of the band broke down equipment, bragged on solos, shot craps; he went outside, knelt behind the bus to count his small treasure. He was relacing his shoe when the emergency brake slipped. In the emergency room, he woke to beg his uncle to peek under the bed. Was the shoe there? The old man knelt, stood grinning with the wrong shoe. Later the orderly told him he'd tossed the right shoe—still attached to the foot—into the incinerator.

These days quarters are tossed at his feet from the iron balconies of hotel bars. Dollar bills slip into his upturned hat like crumpled paper flowers from the fingers of passing blondes. Small change falls toward him with the same will that sends him hobbling through streets cobbled with glass and cigarette butts to reheat a crock full of yesterday's red beans and rice.

All day his soul—taking the shape of whatever songs the dollars requested—flew like a tethered bird past the tourists' heads to beat at the shuttered second and third stories of nearby buildings. Now he settles the guitar like a guest, a visiting angel, in the chair across the table. He lays down the cane and dingy hat, unstraps the sweat-darkened leg. Once more his soul rises, a small wreath of rice steam, through shutter slats to the inexhaustible mist of the river two blocks away.

ENEMIES

Jugglers set down oranges and striped batons, greet banjo and harmonica players with nicknames, slaps on the hand. The street performers meet after the morning's first rainshower to protest laws limiting the noise they make, the crowds they attract.

The plaza's wet flagstones reflect a tattered human rainbow: mimes coy in whiteface, wigs, frayed pastel leotards; a fire-wizard, robe sleeves stitched with faded flames; the one-man band, hunched under his mother-of-pearl bass drum. A toothless black tap dancer distributes day-old rolls donated by the baker whose coffee the street people drink since he gives free refills. Taking a cue from the TV cameraman—who squints into his eyepiece, circling, framing unusual angles—tourists pull out black plastic cameras. They grin, shift from foot to foot and wait for a good shot.

The organizer—a violinist with orange beard and thick, jumpy eyebrows—resembles an old poster describing the Red Menace, tacked up in a washroom where employees shared a cigarette, murmured complaints. The orange-bearded man recites grievances they have all suffered—if not in this city, some other: nightsticks waved in the face, tubas and unicycles confiscated like weapons, a drunk-tank floor glazed with the piss of winos. Applause rises around him like pigeons taking off and lighting a few feet away.

"We have the Constitution," he insists. "Now we fight City Hall." A clown mimes being punched silly by someone invisible. He's not the only one made uneasy by the prospect of making bigger enemies. Fidgety in harlequin suits, twin Asian acrobats stare at a thin curtain of mist coming down between the buildings. The Mexican contortionist fiddles with his straitjacket's rusty straps. A real scuffle erupts between a straw-hatted trumpeter and the wino grabbing his trumpet: "I can show you a thing or two about the blues," he shouts. "I spent New Year '68 in Vietnam." The tourists laugh, it's a good performance.

Insulted, a few performers back off, disperse toward jealously protected streetcorners as the harangue turns toward committees, petitions, and press conferences. Tired, distracted, they wonder whether their next performance will be the last. You can tell they'll hitchhike to other towns upriver, fight the laws and shopkeepers with all they've got: beat-up accordion, disappearing-egg trick, pantomimes of ridicule and disillusionment.

WALKING STICKS

The local art critic in the white linen suit prefers a slim stiletto of ivory carved with monkeys and guardian demons; the loan officer in charcoal pinstripes prefers a black-lacquered crook. Most women stick with shoulder bags, to which they entrust portable fortunes: snapshots of a daughter at one, a son at seven; coupons crumpled around a paper clip; lottery tickets, movie stubs, all the immaterial power of five nicked credit cards. But occasionally you see a stick handled by a woman in tweed slacks and bulky fisherman's sweater, a psychotherapist or professor of anthropology. Swinging a long twisted staff of applewood bought in some alley off Bourbon Street, she strides the grimy levee as though it leads into a Vermont pasture of broomstraw and foxfire.

October light sweeps downriver, clears fog out of the willows and sycamores: your great-aunt told you a good walk cures almost anything. Where you grasp a walking stick will set the arc that paces your day. Think of it as a pendulum that sweeps seconds around the axis of eternity, propelling minutes into hours and hours toward the end of Sunday afternoon.

The hiker returns to her kitchen simmering with the garlicky fragrance of white bean soup. What occurred to her on this day's circular pilgrimage bears repeating, but not in the words she uses at work, or at the shopping mall. As though someone else had prepared the dinner awaiting her she smiles, settles the staff back in its tall clay vase by the door. There its deer head carved of applewood rests among other local powers with which her hand has aged: ebony lion, brass griffin, the sweat-tarnished silver fox missing one red glass eye.

DEVOTION

A woman stamps the mud off her boots and asks the candlemaker to build a candle the exact height and weight of her son. It seems the saint has answered her prayer: the boy broke off a worrisome affair with a woman eight years older than he.

"It has to be five feet nine inches, a hundred sixty-nine pounds, and white," she says. The candlemaker demurs, he can make one that tall but not that heavy. Not unless he constructs a special cypress mold—very expensive. She doesn't want to know the cost; she's promised the saint, she can't cheat him. The candlemaker takes out his pencil anyway and begins making estimates—lumber, paraffin, and does she want a special fragrance added?

Outside, the downspouts are full of a drumming rain. Korea is wet like this, and colder. Her boy hasn't written since boot camp and now he's there, sleeping, she hopes, in a dry bunker behind the lines. She wishes the saint had separated them in some other way. But she won't light a candle that smells of gardenia or sweet bay.

"Pine," she says, remembering the sap that oozed from the wormy planks drying in her father's shed, the resinous pause of his hands on the Bible: "Make it pine."

LYE

Soapmaking is almost forgotten, like the sugarcane splits that used to prop up clotheslines dripping with sheets, work shirts, Sunday tablecloths. Once each neighborhood had its own cane vendor: he hauled cane one certain way, the rhythm of his shout was a signature. And each neighborhood had a child blinded by lye, led to and from church school by an unmarried aunt or—if it happened on the boulevard of raised houses—a fat maid in starched white clothes.

Still fat but white-haired now, the woman fans herself on her back stoop, close to the leap and crackle of flames licking fatwood. Heat or cold, three days before each full moon she lights a fire in her dirt-yard and heats Red Devil in a scarred iron pot. The lye melts: she adds five pounds of kitchen grease—catfish, chicken, pork—and little snapped bones, for marrow. The grease has to be animal fat, to restore belly-skin stretched by labor, kill ringworm, improve bad hair after eczema. It'll pull anything out of the skin that doesn't belong there.

In her apron there's sassafras, purple basil, rose petals rubbed to a filé—tossed in, with a hummed line from a hymn, during stirring. Once it sticks like a heavy jelly to the paddle, it's ready for the pantry—you have to almost forget it, growing hard and white below jars of okra and green tomato pickle. Her grown daughters buy soap off the discount shelves. Only old people who don't want to forget the smell of hardship buy her soap. And twice a week she takes a bar of it to a nursing home for the blind, to one certain man who refuses to be bathed by anyone but her. It has to be her soap, her hands.

To think that the thing that softens his rheumatic joints could have burned the eyesight right out of him. She remembers how his father drove down to the river after church, took off his silk derby, and shot himself. Every Saturday after that she had to bleach and starch her uniform for the formal Sunday walk. Nobody but her thought it ridiculous: the whippet-thin white mother, composed in black with a black parasol; herself, fat, black, and determined to be merry in starched whites; and the boy stretched between them, blind smile tugged this way and that, like a small shirt drying in the wind and sun.

DIRT YARDS

A chinaberry tree smothers everything beneath its thick skirts—pansies, tiger lilies, even crabgrass. Plant five around a house: the angry noise of mowing recedes from year to year, like a father's hairline. He'd sit on the porch steps sweating bourbon, and curse the city: eight miles away, edging closer. "Smoke signals," he called the smudge of industry on the horizon: "It's like war."

Shelling beans in the rocker, you thought a new white skirt would solve everything. Why shouldn't the city come to you, if he wouldn't let you go to it? So the city kept coming. But it allowed the old man to die before the first 7-Eleven appeared at the end of the road. You earned his house but no husband in the years when having a husband mattered.

Across the bridge wetlands are burned off and filled in: flattopped condos with fake mansards, asphalt parking, pampas grass. Green herons disappear, pigeons replace them. The city hasn't reached you yet. But the closer it gets, the staler and cheaper it seems. This winter it sent a token: a skeletal Christmas tree washed up in the lake's gray wind. Tinsel stuck in your shoelaces as you kicked it back in.

Hungry generations of mockingbirds still thank you each night for hiding their young in chinaberry foliage. All summer cicada-song creaks from one tree to the next—an old rope hammock sagging under a pregnant woman in her third trimester. The scallop-back chair parked against the trunk stays cool to your forearms and hams, even in dog days when turning your head too fast brings on a sweat. One day everyone around you will be bought out and gone: the Jehovah Witness neighbor, her boy whose three crippled motorcycles lean against ground-dragging live oak boughs, her bald brother with his tea glass full of cigar ash and gin.

And for what—another acre of condos, fast-food chicken, photomats, and video stores strung on a necklace of sulphur streetlights. Still you mean to hang on in the middle of it. Let the blacktop and edged lawns come. You'll still slowly waltz the soft hearth broom around the clean dirt-yard. Sweep up the pine's worthless gold dust. Sweep your own gray hairs among the threads of Spanish moss that will fall off a little faster in suburban air.

PIGEONS

He could pick them off the railroad trestle with a .22 rifle, shooting from creosote-smeared sleepers over the river: pigeon-wings sleepily unfolded in the sixty-foot drop. Sometimes turtles converged on the wreck of feathers, tugged it under the molasses-thick water; sometimes the dead bird spun in the current, a drowned woman's Sunday hat.

He was eight. He'd just seen an old rotogravure where the boy Audubon, sitting on an oak-stump, wept over the first dove he shot. That didn't prevent the man, stinking of buckskin and bear-greased hair, from killing every bird he ever drew: the snail-eating kite, for one—a fistful of sawdust packed in shellacked feathers. The Double Elephant Folio sat on a gateleg table in great-uncle's study as proof: you could finance a whole life in the wild simply by keeping a record of what you shot.

The pigeons napped, bobbed: he shot one, the rest clattered away. Then he closed his eyes to let them return to the rusty iron roost. They closed the dead-bird gap, heads bobbing. He reloaded. What was worse—his bored cruelty? pigeon stupidity? Falling made them beautiful: to suddenly relax, spin sleepily toward the lukewarm shimmer. He wanted to fall like that, but a fall like that would have killed him. So he got pigeons to fall.

He doesn't expect his wife to understand. He shot three or four dozen at most—nothing like those Sundays in the last century: dozens of families in corn-stubble shot the bird-clotted sky, brought down wagonloads of passenger pigeons. He once studied a passenger pigeon in a mansion turned state museum. Cocked to one side, its frazzled head stared from a bell-jar perch at a larger bell jar containing a ticker-tape machine. Between the two he stood as though any minute the ticker would wake to click out an epitaph for a century of extinctions: the prairie white with buffalo ribs, cypress swamps full of the ghost-drumming of ivory-billed woodpeckers.

His boy-rifle, a short bolt-action with a stock of baseball-bat ash and a scroll of wrought iron for a trigger-guard, stands with old putters and shoehorns in the back of his closet. In the last twenty-five years he has killed almost nothing: cockroaches, mice, one alley cat with the rabid staggers. A houseboat, a clean little grocery, no debts, yard bordered with peonies and irises: all his, all he is.

Sometimes he can hear, over the air conditioner's hiss, the mating song of mourning doves. Behind the cash register, he stares up: they gather on the grocery's gravel roof. That's how he wants it now—doves walking over him, four descending disembodied syllables, *Oh no, no, no.*

ORANGES

Wetplate photographs of oranges forever deny the truth in oranges held close to the eye. How many thousands of teardrop cells are packed in the cottonthread pulp? Tear into the skin: tiny acid explosions spray from its pores. You've set off the combustions of a personal sun.

The artillery major made his reservists spend Sunday morning unloading two boxcars of mortar rounds, neatly pyramiding them in each sandy emplacement of the river-fort, because a famous Atlanta photographer had gotten off the same Army train earlier in town. The major even allowed the reservists to fire ten rounds at noon and shout cheers, on the chance that the photographer might guess a Union gunboat had been engaged, and be lured from his champagne and *pompano en papillote*.

At two the major let the reservists go and entered his tent to complain to his diary. Then with his sabre he divided an orange into four sections and walked out. A snowy egret alighted on a sandbag to delouse itself. The major tossed it an orange rind. Startled, the egret shook its plumes and rose, squawking downriver past idle enemy siegeboats.

And the photographer? All he wanted was to wash out an aftertaste of fish. Champagne-giddy, he found this stack of oranges and thought of Seville, Valencia. Cities of fruit and passionate women. He had grown prosperous and bored in the portrayal of regimental officers vacantly pretending to relax around a blurry Negro with a banjo. For a moment he forgot the gray limits of his skill and tried to catch the essential glow of oranges. Exposed to his black-draped apparatus, they darkened into steel glare and shadow.

Consider the engineer who, after eating pomegranate, designed the hand grenade (also affectionately known as a pineapple). But this pyramid of steel-toned oranges? It's as though arsenals owed all their order to the pride of a fruit-seller: apron pressed, head slick with Macassar, solemn as a drill corporal. Long-range shells laid like cucumbers, carrots. Grenades braided into belts like garlics. Mortar rounds like grapefruit, cantaloupe. Honeydew made iron by men determined not to let small pleasures of ripeness and harvest obstruct hard thinking on the difficult business of siege and blockade, the laws of trajectory and fuse-timing.

A WELL-REGARDED MAN

The general shuts himself into the rented room overlooking a courtyard littered with frayed banana leaves. January: the landlady expects rain. She sets out pots of rosemary among the weedy tiles. The fresh sheaf of stationery at his elbow may turn out to be a memoir that will justify his recent defeats. Just now he remembers the pot of coffee his first wife would set on the floor tiles outside the study. Locked inside, a youthful colonel, he went over Napoleon's tactical errors. It was their second child, the girl, that killed her. Nevertheless her father still sends him a yearly bushel of salted pecans from a grove famous for the death of an English general, whose aides buried his viscera among trampled pecan hulls, shipped the corpse home in a keg of rum.

On the courtyard's borders he can see tatters of swamp iris, wild ginger, fern planted by slaves of the auctioneer who built this house. When he ordered the first shot of the war to be fired on a fort commanded by a West Point friend, his second wife—one of nine sisters known locally as the Muses—wrote that his goatee was showing up in enlistment lines across the city. He learned the names of swamp plants during a low-country retreat: news of her funeral came in over the wire. Often he forgets the second stillborn girl's name.

What if he said nothing of arranging the final surrender, wrote instead about the dollar and fifteen cents he had left after the ceremony? About peddling a wagon full of dry goods through seven hundred miles of hamlets and dirt farms to pay his way home? On one side of town they say rosemary is for luck. On the other they say for remembrance. He feels lucky that he is almost done with remembering; that his surviving son owns a house where he can go in a few years to die, with its entryway grillwork of two doves bent over a bowl of pomegranates.

A whole afternoon gone. Rain begins to blacken the courtyard without his committing a single word to paper. The landlady knocks brusquely, with a cup of coffee by now lukewarm, her endless story of a husband lost in a minor western campaign. Getting up, he notices the portrait of his first wife still on the floor, leaning face against the wall—as she sometimes did near the end of the killing pregnancy. Not even a million deaths, he thinks, will make the iron doves touch the pomegranates.

TWO TOYSHOPS

1.

The president, two inches of enameled lead dressed in mourning, has removed his stovepipe hat. His hair is brushed back to indicate where the light strikes best. He poses for a black-draped camera that will presently blow off the better part of his head, and start the clock-steps of tiny regimental bands standing at attention on other glass shelves: Black Watch, Brown Shirts, Maximilian's Zouaves, and Green Berets.

When the sun slants at a certain angle, a single shopwindow can condense history, flash it at the passerby. Next in the parade, a Model T bearing Edison and Rockefeller. A Panzer tank with Rommel locked in stiff-arm salute. A few reptilian Cadillacs full of the high-hatted inheritors of exhausted colonies. Much can be rehearsed with toys, much explained.

Is death an incandescent light that goes off in the head? the final bit of lead bumping down a frayed conveyor belt? It must be a cold, small knowledge, leaden as these effigies. But the president is no longer in a position to say.

Behind him the procession continually unwinds: the Raja's jeweled elephant, tractor trailers laden with olive-green missiles, the dead Cid strapped to his Arabian charger, Philistine generals gripping the gilt rails of their chariots. A multitude of flags, no toy children anywhere. Real ones aren't allowed to touch anything here. One little hand can start a corrosion that will spread from piece to piece.

It's no mistake that the president's photographer wears a surgeon's white coat. Imagine him removing the black hood, lead feet leaping to attend his fainting leader beneath crossed swords, the painted white puffs of the rifle salute.

2.

There is a world where one frog is poised to fiddle while another smiles over his flute. The rest prepare to drum and jig around the chief frog, who wears a crimson fez. He'll give the downbeat by stamping on a tiger skin just bigger than himself. It's an old world cast, not surprisingly, in iron.

A tabby cat plans her Ping-Pong serve, the Siamese tenses for the return. Passersby are amused by the black terrier who balances on cross-country skis. But who can pay what the rum-drinking pigs demand for the pleasure of their company, their picnic table covered with dominos? Every year the past grows more costly.

The six-inch tin housefly towers over an inch-tall bronze lion, a rabbit reads the funnies atop the wolf's frilly parasol—dreams of subversion, comprehended perfectly in the laughter of children. Mothers tug them toward errands and supper, their condensed breath fades from the window. The few buyers are old, haggle half-heartedly with the shopkeeper.

Is it her immense hairdo, piled on the pink skull like white spun sugar, the ticking of her brittle, gold-nailed fingers on a glass case? What makes them pull out their wallets sooner than they meant to? Surrounded by the iron vestiges of a century's childhoods, she studies the customer, selects the animal that will find the path to his underworld: a blind sparrow with its white cane, or bulldog gazing stolidly over its shoulder, waiting for the new master to catch up.

She stiffens with oracular dignity as the money is spread before her. She attends many funeral auctions, knows the stories of figurines pried from rigid hands. Knows which animals she'll see again. Handing one over, she murmurs, "Take care of him for me"—the black terrier that will motionlessly ski through another decade of cupboard dust across town on its pilgrimage back to her.

The Streets of the Muses

EUTERPE

Higher than any nearby business, the dead royal palm still commands attention, fronting a row of tall white empty houses. Poor people lived here: their windows broadcasted a chorus of soul, jazz, salsa, blues stewed in peppers and fatback. The cries of women echoed off unwashed fences with a desperate dignity. After school, children brought to the street the ancient chants for hopscotch, double Dutch rope-skips.

The house of the palm was last owned by a river-captain's illegitimate daughter. She settled in with her dozen-odd cats when it grew clear that no white suitor would pick her. In the half-light that belongs to milkmen and birdsong, there would sometimes float from her bedroom window the scratchy voice of a long-dead tenor. It was the only record she had of the Italian who spent a few nights of his American tour on her father's paddleboat, Baton Rouge to Cairo. The only proof that he had once dedicated to her an aria from *La Bohéme*. It had happened in the stateroom after dinner, hundreds of well-dressed white people watching. She watched their shock multiply in Venetian mirrors on each wall, then heard her own heart in tempo with the ship's great paddle. His high C made the wineglass hum in her hand.

Only a few months ago she could be seen out on her porch, in a faded satin gown, filling a porcelain milk-saucer for each arthritic cat. Each Sunday, summer or winter, she would wear a fox stole to the local park and sit on a bench humming loudly. She peeled lapfuls of pecans for squirrels and pigeons, scarcely regarding the hoots of boys on red bikes, the real estate speculator poking at his handheld calculator.

Even in a good wind, the palm won't let go of its dry gray fronds or salty roots. They'll have to drag it out with a tow chain. Mimosas spill through her fence, they still withdraw at a touch. Even on overcast days her four o'clocks bloom at four o'clock.

TERPSICHORE

The sexual dance of the mayflies finishes, the blood dance of mosquitoes starts whining below the street's crisscrossed power lines. It's the hour when teenage boys practice breaking, rapping under spreading cones of streetlight. Their steps were imported by an older cousin from Harlem. His words, rhymed, chanted, executed with precise slashing moves, guarantee passage into the serious hustle and jive of uptown bars. Across the street, carrying milk and bacon, walks a mother they know and ignore. She had a boy their age last year—he got shot off his bike. Tonight she's trailed by a toddler, also practicing what it takes to keep up.

Between the green and the pink house across the street a drunk snores, head thrown back, on a ripped vinyl chair. Neighbors provide for his nightly journey into stupor, a necklace of mosquito bites rises on his throat. Not long ago he could have shown these boys, the breakers and rappers, something about the buck-and-wing. Once, on the wide sidewalk that connected the great department stores, he was known as the dancing preacher. Children chalked his gangly stick figure on the alley walls of Woolworth's. They chalked up his name beside the lord Jesus, they wrote *Amen.*

When the bites get too bad he wakes, slapping himself, remembering he's no longer welcome. He can see the balcony where, once a week, his old wife lowers the rope-slung plastic bleach bottle containing bills and letters to a taxi driver waiting below. Beneath the balcony are the three garage doors, almost always locked, whose panels are crudely numbered in pencil for some boy's street-game. Seeing it makes him thirsty. Thirsty because he can't help thinking of numbered steel panels in the city morgue. That's where it started going wrong. Where his brother—and who knows who else?—lay unwashed, refrigerated meat gone bad, unclaimed for days on end.

THALIA

Funny how a single block can be prey to housefires. Whitewashed shotgun houses stick up among the sooty hulks like good teeth in rotting gums. In surrounding streets people stand around, smoke, complain how cold it is, how nothing much happens. But one street's idle talk turns into barbed wire a block away. These tenants are taking measures: iron window grilles, Dobermans, concertina wire strung lavish as Christmas tinsel atop their hurricane fences.

The landlord's younger nephew has been seen driving a sportier car than his gas-jockey job can pay for. He laughs like he came into too much money at once, talks up their daughters at the gas station. The landlord's other nephew can joke, smile in ways that put white clients at ease. He sends a generous monthly tithe to the neighborhood freewill tabernacle, though now he lives and worships across the river among the suburbanites he insures.

Meanwhile the block's tenants don't watch the reruns of sitcoms that used to make them laugh so hard, like the fat bus-driver who discovers his pants are on fire, lets out a cross-eyed howl, and crashes right through his flimsy dining-room wall. If the TV is on now, it's the only thing laughing. These evenings women send out for dinner, men stand guard at barred windows. North, the street leads to the housing projects; south it disappears among glassy office towers. And the towers are moving. Behind wrecking crews, with tumorous indifference, the towers are migrating north, block by block, out of the city's congested plazas.

POLYMNIA

Draped with hundreds of keys, the wooden St. Peter looks down at a tin bowl stuffed with slips of folded paper. The priest, in his unheated apartment behind the main altar, breakfasts on cold rice and peas. It's Tuesday, St. Lucy's day: he pockets only petitions to heal blindness and eye disease.

He's sure there will be a special plea from the diabetic lacemaker, who won't give up her chocolate truffles and mocha cremes. The doctor has ordered her to choose between sugar and her livelihood. Instead, she has begun to accept skirts and trousers for alteration. "I can hem with both eyes shut if I have to," she writes, enclosing the key to her dead husband's bedroom. She trusts St. Lucy will unlock the mercy of heaven.

Hasn't the priest seen cures stranger than this? —The two cousins whose faces, scalded by an exploding whisky still, grew smooth and white again after they surrendered to him the keys to their fast cars and a bootleg warehouse? Once a week he dusts their chipped profiles. Dozens of trusses, neck braces, plaster lungs and feet and hearts hang along the walls, above rows of identical plaques carved with the word *Thanks*. Some donors he has buried; others he hasn't seen since they dropped off the replicas of their ailments. He himself is guilty of taking an offering not meant for him.

Twelve years ago at this table, late at night, he sat unfolding supplications for an end to this daughter's asthma or that uncle's stinginess. A torn piece of butcher's paper slid out from the wadded envelopes. On it was scratched the word *Fire*. A tingling began at the base of his spine, spread until his hair and fingertips prickled. In a gusty moment he became God's firewood. Decades of catechism and dull ministry charred, fell away. The rest of his life would be a controlled burn.

That night he sewed the butcher's paper into the breast pocket of his habit. The following Sunday he stopped charging fees for candles and perpetual lights. He also stopped heating his rooms. The prayers, the keys, the dusty relics, and the lacemaker's chocolates all point to the fire. Fire is enough. Some cold mornings it's enough to be lacing his shoes and feel the hidden scrap, the password, crackle a little against his chest.

URANIA

The math teacher feels a sequence of high primes as a smile spreading through his chest and arms. He climbs three flights, feet counting each stairstep, toward his bachelor efficiency. In fifteen years, nothing inside has changed except the books piled at the foot of the bed. Each pebble he crunches on the driveway, coming and going, is itself an extraordinary calculus. The scuppernong grapes he bought once last summer he made into an abacus on the tablecloth. He balanced his checkbook, then ate the abacus in thirty bites.

The first day of class each year he holds up both hands, fingers spread: "Your hand is the measure of all things," he announces. Then, baby-voiced, counts on his fingers by ones. Before their teenage laughter dies back he's demonstrating sixteenth-century finger symbols for five-digit numbers. He likes to tease: peels a hard-boiled egg while asking why love equals zero in tennis. Pours sand through a tiny funnel over his desk globe as he explains how Archimedes reckoned, in grains of sand, what the universe amounted to. Each year when he declares there is no final number, the parents complain—especially those who believe in millennium, in the date 4004 B.C.

His third-floor neighbor, a church choir alto, accounts herself among the saved. She no longer needs to open the hymnal to confirm which of three hundred melodies the preacher calls for by number. Her porous hipbones and varicose veins require a great-nephew's help on Sundays, because there's no elevator; she'll have to enter a rest home soon. When the teacher's own arthritis flares, he wonders if he'll last into his nineties like his great-aunt—who ended up playing with Christmas ribbons on a TV tray. She spooled up red and blue shine between her fingers, let it unravel. "I'm making beauty," she would announce. One visit she turned the teacher into her brother, killed in Cuba, 1898; another time he became her son, taken by influenza in 1918. Or she didn't see him at all, but kept arguing with Teddy, with Woodrow and the Kaiser. Her mind the slippery mess of color she let flow through her fingers.

Elsewhere there are whole peoples who know nothing of zero, who live and die and never count past two. Sometimes the teacher can calm his fear of mindless sick old age: his feet count steps from classroom to cafeteria to teachers' lounge; on the sofa, eyes closed, he resumes his lifelong exploration of eight-digit primes. There is no end of numbers. But the end of his years will be a number any child of five can count—by ones, seated on the curb, as hearse and cortege pass—in a singsong voice.

ERATO

Love isn't love that excludes the crippled spinster's feeling for her crutches, polished by the ephemeral oil of her hands. Resting on the stoop of a boarded-up laundromat, she turns them and turns them in the light. The sunlight has as much to do with the Korean war veteran wino who lies on a park bench—white-haired rheumatic chest bared to the morning warmth—as with the young mother who picks up his bottle-shards, so her blind boy can play in the sand. And what sunlight gives, sand accepts: blind digging fingers, glassy alcoholic litter. Under a live oak, the sand holds the undisturbed impression of a woman's back and naked buttocks, pressed deep by the weight of another body.

The corner of the blue laundromat brightens right where it proclaims *Judy Cooter I Love You.* The boy who passes it each week to fetch oil of cloves for his grandmother sometimes skips, sometimes drags his feet, but never fails to mouth the words. And his future? Like a black pigeon, banking its wings around a corner of his school, vanishing up the avenue to the river. But today the park is full of pigeons finding what they need. And tonight his grandmother—after rubbing her gums—will let him sit up late to watch the night-blooming cereus unfold its aromatic white mystery. The rest of the year it lies dormant, a souvenir of times when her casual smile was enough to make sailors walk toward her father's blue house. They came at noon, singing to themselves in all that light, carrying bright potted plants from Brazil and Tenerife.

MELPOMENE

She lost sixteen out of twenty-six in wind-rattled shacks on one Delta sharecrop farm or another. A body can't fill a hundred-pound sack of cotton all day and hope to bear every baby it carries. The first three seized her like snakebite: she'd lean against a mule, yell, the grandmothers and little girls would unstoop from the dirt and come running. The boss might allow a box of tea, two days off.

After the fourth one lived, the rest that she lost hurt less than a rooster pecking a palmful of corn. One miscarried while she stood beating biscuit dough on the windowsill: twitched inside, ran down the back of her knees. It was the sweat of mothering, that's all. She had too little time to believe much besides the redbird broadcasting from the deep shade of the chinaberry.

Here in the city she feels like a fern scrabbling to root between bricks of the Bible Baptist bell tower. Her dead husband looks as trapped in the framed Polaroid grin on her dresser as he was under the tractor in a cotton-corroded gully. Her dimes and dollar bills can't help the nine surviving boys whose lives are an atlas of goodbyes—Memphis, Savannah, Chicago, Berlin, she can't keep track. Her job in a laundry busies her hands with blouses, skirts, even gowns and long soft formal gloves.

If she can last, keep praying, one those boys might produce a girl who'd fill clothes as carefully washed and folded as these. But on the walk home to her room, she wants to drop into an alley patch of flowering vetch and wild chrysanthemum. Wants to lie down and let country grass heal over her swollen ankles and nosebleeds. Her arms are heavy as unleavened bread, in her belly there's a stale weight that buttermilk doesn't ease, that the Sunday tambourine doesn't lift.

She pines for the taste of Yazoo City clay, the wet brown sacks of it her husband scooped out of irrigation ditches when the thing in her belly was starving her. How young she was to let that pain take hold. Between cotton rows she lay: grandmothers wiped her bloody legs, nodded, clucked. Behind them, lint-headed girls peered down from the Mississippi clouds—the eyes of daughters, round as blackberries lit by blackberry flowers.

CLIO

A generation ago lakeside laborers dug up an entire Choctaw necropolis. Tin buckets clattered with the bones of princesses. Soon another amusement arcade crawled above the water on immense stilts. Its pier, strung with yellow bulbs, gave off the profitable aroma of catfish and doughnuts.

The history of Choctaws, of rice and cotton and slavery, makes schoolchildren drowsy. Some fight off the drowse, the teacher-drone, by planning which pinball or video game they'll challenge tonight at the arcade—the wet-dream motorcycle blond, or the flying ace whose jet carries them so far, so fast. Stroll through the arcade and its cargo of garish video noise at night: you can't hear the waves below the pier, but they keep coming in.

Without the sound of waves, of water moving, some people can't get to sleep. One, a barge-mate who only wanted to live before his time: to pilot a riverboat, pole bayous on a pirogue loaded with furs—identities he assumed from old books. For twelve years he's made the daily stinkboat run: out to the Gulf, barge piled with the city's refuse. A paperback of Twain or Fenimore Cooper was jammed in his back pocket to read on the way back, after pitching overboard the last debris of chickenbones, rotted fruit, smashed toys.

Where does his insomnia come from? Living on this hot street, his father-in-law's street, so far from the lake and the river? or that trip when his pitchfork nosed through the rot and caught the eyehole of a human skull? At night he misses the day-sound of waves, their repetitions, soothing, wordless. Hard not to lie awake guessing where your bones might end up: in a tin bucket for schoolkids to steal, or strewn piecemeal in a Gulf current, in the cloudy tonnage of garbage going down where the big channel catfish wait.

Tonight he continues with the history of the river. It's a yellowed volume, long outdated by versions less dependent on legend and hearsay. Still he prefers the feel of its frayed leather. He opens it to

Marquette's fever in the canoe, his burial among the Indians—a page that bears the imprimatur of a flattened silverfish.

CALLIOPE

For three nights a cry flew past the upper windows of a boardinghouse edging the park. For three days—breakfast, tea, and supper—boarders met to trade explanations. "It's the spirit of yellow fever orphans," insisted the seamstress twins, passing the deviled eggs. But they themselves were orphans. Anything that bewildered them they blamed on baby abandonment. The postman's widow—a flagrant hypochondriac—said through her handkerchief that the apparition cried "Oh doctor!" in an old-lady voice. Death, she thought, was having a joke at her expense. The bookkeeper swallowed a deviled egg and looked around. A girl, he confessed, had hoarsely whispered "I love you!" through his bedroom shutters. When wings beat the shutter, he realized it was the Tempter talking.

By the fourth day strangers argued the spirit's identity up and down the streetcar line, leading to several fistfights and at least one fractured skull. That night, reported the neighborhood policeman, a cry issued directly from the lips of the park statue. (This statue—the nation's first one of a woman who was not a goddess, muse, or symbol—commemorated an Irish scrubwoman. She had invested her thrift in a bakery, donated its profits to the city's orphans.) One newspaper declared the statue wept over the failure to find a cure for TB. The other daily seized the opportunity to bewail children left fatherless by the government's foolish adventures in the Philippines. When the policeman admitted—he was in a saloon, collecting for the widow-and-orphan fund—that he'd also heard the statue shriek "Doctor, I love you!", both newspapers solemnly deplored the drunkenness of policemen.

On the fifth day, a Sunday, clowns stepped off the streetcar and waddled toward the haunted park. A man in a ringmaster's top hat, red vest, and cutaway coat followed. Behind him a dwarf hauled an empty wicker cage almost as large as himself. After three blocks they were trailed by a crowd suspicious this was all ordained by the Antichrist. "I will demonstrate," the ringmaster declared, "once and for all what spirit has troubled your peace." He approached the statue and bowed. The clowns deployed in a semicircle, the dwarf opened the cage. The ringmaster raised both arms and blew on a tiny silver whistle.

Out of the oaktrees behind the statue flew a large crimson parrot, a runaway, a circus star. "Hello, precious!" the ringmaster shouted. Disheveled, half-starved, it landed at his feet. He bowed, the parrot bowed back. "Oh doctor!" it cried. "Oh doctor, I love you!"

Toward a Bad End

REVIVAL

Any sharecropper can give you half the history of the South in two verses of delta blues. The rest he hums, squatting to roll a cigarette in the shade of his mule. History is the yellowed newspapers that insulate his bedroom and living room and kitchen, which are the same room. Steak was 37 cents a pound, hamburger 24 cents—that's how the city talked about itself. Out here a string of fish cost a handful of worms and a dozen mosquito bites. A good pointing dog could fill his coat pockets with quail. He had a bush full of hen-eggs, two hogs a year, all the work he could bear. Saturday night blues, Sunday gospel.

Hitler? Bad news far away. He'll tell you his overseer was worse because he was mean right here, daylight to dark, every day. The man wore yellow riding pants though he drove the property in a no-door truck, kept a pencil-lead mustache, hated getting dirty. His jowls swelled red and purple when black men talked back, when they threw down cotton sacks to catch a freight to Chicago. The week of the A.M.E. Zion revival he drove off the levee. When his drowning was confirmed, the revivalists started a slow spiritual, but as it speeded up there was no hiding what all the clapping was for. Even the catfish and hushpuppies tasted better that night.

Any sharecropper can tell you: one bad white man with land can spoil it for a whole parish. He holds out his cigarette hand with its scarred pink palm: like a goddamn infected splinter, he swears. He's never met a white who'd do a black man much good, but the land bank's white and he—he knows how to keep his peace. Too much shouting and stealing in cities, north or south. No wood thrush song to make darkness holy—just big trucks rumbling everyone awake before dawn, after midnight.

Out here he keeps a clean-swept yard, a chinaberry tree, and a cane chair to pull up under it. His black and tan hound can fetch up a rabbit to fatten the stew, can lay it right at your feet. The hound gets up off the cool chinaberry dirt and stretches, eyeing you. Are you staying to eat? Two fields over, his brother's wife lets the screen door wheeze and slap behind her. In the reddening air she raises her head, hollers *Supper!*

BONEMEAL

The river was good enough for dead sheep and deer—not for dead white people. But dig a grave? That was waste labor. Everywhere water lay waiting six inches underfoot. Earth burial meant having to bore holes in the bottom of the coffin, set it afloat in the waterlogged hole, make a slave or two stamp on it until it started sinking. A colonial trader might choose an old Indian shell mound barely grassed over: his corpse would fill it like an enormous spoiled oyster.

After the Revolution citizens were buried aboveground: in hives of sealed and whitewashed brick if they had money; if they didn't, in shallow, stacked ovens built into the city's ramparts—rented long enough for the flesh to decay. To pacify the swarm of souls awaiting judgment, survivors brought chrysanthemums on All Saints Day. In new winter fashions, the well-to-do received callers before the family tomb. Sausages, pickles, and orange wine were laid out on white iron tables and benches; aunts and great-aunts took turns bedding mums in marble urns. The poor were limited to cheap glass vases in which they stuck paper roses colored with pokeberry juice.

Fear of yellow fever made young people create burial societies. Members held raffles and dances to finance tombs big enough for a hundred bachelors, a hundred spinsters. Less and less frequently, a backhoe bites into a layer of bone marking where the fever wagons dumped other epidemic victims. After the Civil War, the racetrack bankrupted and was reformed into the biggest necropolis: Vermont granite, Carrara marble, stunned angels on every other roof.

Here, conchs flank the doorways of the vaults, the oyster-shell paths are bordered with overlapped scallops. Here, like calls to like—as in the oyster bar where a cabdriver leans back, teeth parted as though for a kiss, and lifts oyster after tongue-soft oyster onto his tongue. His grandfather's grandfather died at Shiloh; he in turn had a grandfather killed in Napoleon's autumn campaign, 1809. In spring 1810, Austrian farmers harvested thousands of skeletons. A London manufacturer bought the whole lot, ground it into feed for English cattle and corn.

A spoonful of bonemeal and the chrysanthemums fill their squat white urns with bronze blooms. So a pregnant woman swallows white calcium pills to rebuild the strength the unborn child sucks from her bones daily. So birth takes death into its mouth and eats, and is nourished. In each cemetery, a century of southern light has turned the cheap, once-clear vases violet: the color of humility, repentance, of love united with pain.

EYES OF THE SWORDFISH

In these three blocks the quiet is prerevolutionary: it rises out of the cool brick streets, seeps from the terra-cottas of the Creole houses, tall, close-packed, shuttered all day. The only way you know it's noon is when Our Lady of Pompeii spews out its host of pigtails and pleated tartan skirts. Two or three shutters will push open then: maids quietly instructed to listen, to hear whether certain daughters are shouting words they're forbidden to whisper at home. The girls' games are confined to the length of the church, a street blocked off by police barricades. But a kickball will sometimes carom off the church wall out of the neighborhood, into the retail street.

Without leaving his milk-crate perch, the Korean florist swings one leg into the gutter to halt the ball. Always he buffs it on his apron before returning it to the nun whose umpire's whistle is her sole piece of earthly authority. But when a girl is sent for the ball, he invariably leads her past the barricade to select something—a blue tulip, a mottled carnation. The florist has no daughters himself. He claps his hands softly as she carries ball and flower aloft, back to the hoots and giggles of her opponents and friends.

The fishmonger, against whose window-grate the ball sometimes bounces, doesn't trust a man who forces flowers on little girls whose language he barely speaks. In his front window's display bin he kneels in fresh ice to wrestle a seven-foot swordfish into place. He jams its bill into the dough-soft wood of the window molding, wipes blood-crust off the gills. By Friday evening only fins and the pronged head will remain. Just now it's perfect—each eye barely beginning to cloud over.

The fishmonger doesn't trust little girls either. Their giggles evolve into throaty laughter as they discover all the other things their bodies can do. He has a daughter who's practicing being a woman three cities upriver: less and less she comes home to appease his indignation over her money troubles. His wife is no help—if anything she's getting more girlish herself. Last weekend she shared the courtyard's iron loveseat with the girl, getting advice on clothes, on hair color and facials. He bent over the kitchen sink, trying to rid his hands of squid-smell, and watched his wife whisper to his daughter, woo her. He had to remind himself it was water, not laughter, pouring out of the faucet.

Now he brushes the ice from his knees, peers up at a flat cloud that might catch on the cross-tipped steeple and tear. The neighborhood is best at evening: he can put on his dark suit and walk, hands clasped behind his back. Can slow his pace until each step becomes a measure of dignity that other men see, and nod at. He's glad his daughter is gone. And in five minutes all the little soprano shouts will subside through the church-school's stone passageway: back to the enforced silence of multiplication tables, teachings of the desert fathers. He turns to uncrate another hundredweight of squid. How fast can a swordfish can go underwater? For this one, it wasn't fast or deep enough.

TAGS

The cat is a little smaller today. Thanks to the vans loaded with strawberries and nectarines, its ruff of black and white blends more into the oily gray of the flea market lot. Its inner reds are finally black and dry, but still adhesive. The man whose job it is to scrape up animal accidents noted the cat on his clipboard three days ago, but it's not flat enough to satisfy him yet. It had shots, license, a name he's memorized. The cat's tags click in his tag pocket.

He got this job because the other job the city gave him—pruning trees along the streetcar line—ended badly. He'd been young enough to like the noise, chainsaw and wood-chipper. The noise made him talk and laugh more loudly—something he felt a man ought to do anyway: show he wasn't a boy. But this job has always been quiet. Drive around the city, clean up the animal dead. Possums, raccoons were always easy—no one to notify. With dead pets he fetched the remains to the owner, in burlap or a salvaged shoe box, as soon as he could. For years that was his policy—let them know quick, see it and be certain.

But in the last two years the owners all seem to have gotten old. This run-over spaniel or bluepoint Siamese were dinner companions, bedmates, mute and attentive proof, finally, that a man was not talking to himself. More than one widow has made him sit, over weak coffee, comparing snapshots of terrier and husband. The survivor always ends up resembling the one survived, animal, human, it doesn't matter. And his job is to show that now, the survivor is gone, too. That's why he's letting this cat turn into asphalt. He doesn't want to see one more old face pinched with tears, the ugly, ordinary noise of grief starting up in the throat. He's too old to listen to that.

In the morning now he won't even look at his good hand until it's done its job, until it's fixed the fiberglass forearm and dull hook to the other elbow. His good hand has begun to look too much like his dead mother's hand: like a mother who bends over a stumpy child and buttons his coat, sets his ugly cap on straight. When his real hand looks like that in the morning, by noon it can't hold a coffee cup or write the names and numbers of the new road kills. He has to park the truck and sit on the hand. He has to keep it from taking him back to mother on her front stoop, crying—plucking sawdust from his hair, rifling the bag of bloody leaves and splinters at her feet for the one thing that will never touch her again.

FLAMINGO TONGUE

So long since she knelt—since she was small enough to kneel and hide—in marshgrass, watching brown pelicans tilt and divebomb the mullet. Which end of the island was it? She remembers earthworks above the lagoon, rocky bulwarks thrown up by soldiers and their slaves to stave off an assault on the port upriver. Her father could point out the mounds where the most bluecoats died, could name the generals, the admirals and warships. Better than history he liked flinging his shrimpnet into the shallows. Most days he got nothing more than a rock crab, the satisfaction of fifty near-perfect casts.

In sawgrass she squatted over fiddler crabs—tiny black bodies, huge white claws—performing intricate ritual disputes. When a heron-shadow passed overhead, the ballet of waving claws vanished down wet tunnels. It was shells she wanted, that she cut her knees and hands on sawgrass for. But this was only the river. When father found her a book of old shell-drawings, the names were so strange—who had gotten to name these unbroken, almost imaginary things? Specialists, father said. Men who specialize in shells. In bed she whispered Lightning Whelk, Blood Ark, Lettered Olive, strained to hear the turquoise surf. Sundial, True Tulip: how fine the white sand would feel to her knees.

Twenty-four years a secretary in the urban redevelopment office and she's left the city twice—once for the World's Fair, once for a conference in Washington, D.C. She never really wanted to see those Caribbean islands where shells come from. And those men—thin windy hair, sunfreckled skulls—who give official names to things dead at their feet? She works for specialists like that. She's worked for them for twenty-four years.

If she wants anything it's only herself, small in the brackish reeds. Her father, tirelessly catching nothing in the clear shallows of his own thoughts. The ferment of oyster flats, low tide. The ice cream truck parked lopsidedly on the earthworks, issuing its three scratchy, descending notes like a huge scarred music box. And herself again,

working toes into a mud littered with white claws, making a song—
Lion's Paw, Angel Wing—out of images whose originals she would
never see: Baby's Ear. Flamingo Tongue.

HERMIT CRAB

He used to sell insurance upriver: things change. For years everyone looks like a customer, waiting to be sold—then a voice starts gargling nonsense beneath the sidewalk, or out of a particularly old oak by the backyard gate. His wife went on repotting African violets on the patio, customers kept griping about losing teams and bad government. But the faces started to slip; voices dissolved to a sly white noise. Soon there was nothing there to make sense of.

He quit sleeping. Passing cars began to glare and roar at him. He took to hiding near the waterfront, finally fell asleep on a tied-up barge. When he woke he was lying half-drowned in an acre of shallow oyster beds. The city was gone—all he could see was shells, delta-mud, the saltwater horizon. There was a short dock that began and ended in the water. He crawled under it during the day, climbed up when the sun got low. He didn't try to do any more than that.

A Filipino fisherman found him, oyster-slashed, voiceless with thirst. The fisherman hauled him up to a stilt house full of drying fish, strapped him to a plank bed rigged with mosquito netting. Water was forced past his gargling fear of it, of the hands that funneled it in. He only woke to shake, or yell. At night ghost crabs came up from the sand to scavenge, claws ticking on boards and palmetto fronds. Twice a day the fisherman washed his cuts, spooned fish broth into him.

When he started crying steadily, the fisherman untied him and led him to the dunes. There he pointed out an abandoned concrete tower, once used to spot U-boats. Go there, his smile meant: No other white people have to know. So the man went. He ate glasswort, mud snails, things the Gulf washed up. Sometimes the children—they were all Filipino there—brought a sack of oysters; they sent their laughter first, to warn him to hide.

One day the fisherman translated the name the children had given him: Hermit Crab. He liked the sound in Tagalog, and learned to answer to it. By then he could sit at a social fire, smile, let children touch his beard and laugh. Word traveled upriver: a hermit on the delta, doing penance for the sins of men. He had taken a vow of silence, was wise and simple—maybe even holy. Young white people—long-haired, with backpacks and sleeping bags—started showing up at the tower.

I had a wife in Memphis, he tells them, squatting by his fire in rubber boots and ragged palmetto hat, roasting the liver of a nurse shark that washed up yesterday. They want simplicity? In winter he runs down marsh rabbits, snares ducks and marsh hens; in spring he digs turtle eggs. He's ridden mother turtles out to sea and returned on the backs of porpoises. Holiness? He bares his chest and back, mapped with oyster-shell scars. Seven years Nebuchadnezzar lived like a beast of the fields, he reminds whoever's come to stare. He bites skewered meat and stirs the fire, content with his animal feet and his stench and his Nebuchadnezzar appetite, Filipino godchildren and Gulf wind and a wife in Memphis, maybe.

LUCKY TOBIES

He said, The law is against toby-sellers, don't tell nobody I told you about tobies because the law says I can't. You believe in luck, don't you though? Sure you do! Things don't just happen. That's where tobies come in.

I put lucky things in my tobies—high-john-the-conqueror, five-finger grass, four-leaf clover, a white powder, a black powder, and a pink powder. They cost me plenty. I put two more things in, but I forget them now. Put all these things in a fancy colored bag called a lucky bag, then wrap it in cellophane tied with a pretty ribbon. That keeps the lucky bag clean.

I'd show my toby but that would rob all the luck out of it. A quick peek might not hurt, but like a fool when I changed my pants I left my toby in the wrong pocket. It's a wonder I ain't been all cut up or run over today. My tobies never fail—never fail. You got to put your faith in the toby or you won't get nothing but trifling results.

Here's how I pitch it. "Put up and built by the Seven Sisters in New Orleans, my toby will bring you Honor, Riches, and Happiness. It will help you Win in all Games. Thieves nor Enemies cannot bother you. Hold on to your Loved One. Get anyone you Love. Make your Babies look like you. Protect yourself against all Law. Everything you touch Prospers you and makes you Money. Hold the Bag in your Left hand, blow hot breath on it Three times and see if your Wish don't come to pass before the Seventh day is gone. Keep a Toby on your person at all Times. Just one dollar is all they cost, but they're worth five hundred times more."

The poor white and the poor black folks are my best customers—it ain't because they're dumber than rich folks; the dumb ones are the folks who don't buy tobies to help them. Poor folks need more luck than rich folks—that's why they buy more tobies. I guarantee you won't regret this, he said.

GAMBLERS

A basket of fried calamari, still sizzling, shuts up the mouth from Pittsburgh bragging out the café's open front door. For a few seconds, the flies have the floor. Then empty beer bottles take over, clanking into sacks behind the bar: green glass in one, clear in the other. The sewage pipes, painted black and hung across the ceiling, gurgle at regular intervals.

Men will gamble on how often a drinker gets up to piss, how often he wipes his lips, with which hand. Nobody's drinking? They'll bet on the number of drowned flies in the handicapped urinal, how many times the bartender checks the clock in an hour. Nickel and dime each other to death.

Outside, pedestrians impatiently gauge rates of taxi and bus acceleration along Decatur. They check stoplight intervals, test their running shoes—curb to blacktop, blacktop to curb. Splitting the pedestrians, a bored boy who's stolen his father's Porsche to cruise town on a groundnote of heavy metal. Revved up, revving, he's hunting yellow lights—wants to squeeze those lemons. His chewed-up fingers itch on the radiophone to be WYYY's ninth caller for the Thursday thousand. There's also the shoeshine man who stops every tourist strolling the levee: "A dollar says I can tell you in what county, city, and street you got your shoes."

Big Pittsburgh mouth is touring the south on a stack of twenty dollar bills a foot high, courtesy of his corner bookie. He goes through the breaded squid, two more *cervezas* please, and resumes his harangue about the box theory in playing the daily numbers. Bartender checks the clock for the eighth time since noon: somebody has to buy a round, pay the debt of laughter.

At the bus stop a white-haired man, lugging a string bag of papayas, counts on his rosary to keep him from being infected by the two boys who just used him in the public toilet. And all through the grassless, treeless stretches of raw tract houses that hem the city, people in bathrobes and slippers pad down driveways to check their mailboxes: maybe today it's not a shampoo sample, a Save The Child appeal, but that thin expensive stationery that exclaims in gold 20 Million, Dream Chalet, Rolls Royce. Maybe this time it's not just a come-on, a hook, a sucker punch.

ON DUTY

A harmonica starts up uneasily in the dusk, more like a startled insect than what it is—a kid mouthing his new toy. The tuneless mournful wheeze floats across the river into cypresses, into one barely lit fisherman's shack. The middle-aged man lies on a ruptured sofa beneath the window. He feels no need to peer out over the sill to tell whose boy picks his way barefoot between cypress knees and crawfish mounds, blowing, sucking his handful of tin and wood.

From the way frogs have gone silent downstream, the man knows a night heron has impaled a frog in a shallow pool, has tilted its head back to swallow it. Upstream, a faint bellow and thrashing of water says a bull gator has grabbed something that came to drink—a wild pig, or a fawn. Staring up, the man can see a sliver of last rose light that the ibises ride, over his roof, home to their marsh rookery.

The kid's father used to fish this river. Then he got hooked on offshore oil wages, followed oil to the Alaska pipeline. The mother makes extra money sleeping around. Across the river, the boy is trying to mouth the sound of a disappearing train. The man can hear an old good-bye in that music that he understood first at a south Georgia train station in 1943, when he watched his sharecropper father's red ears vanish in dust and steam. Later, in Italy, on sniper duty in an olive grove, he understood better.

He had fallen asleep in the crotch of a tree. An ocarina woke him. The melody floated up the slope from the stream: it was a Strauss waltz. Tracking it through the scope he saw an enemy helmet bob carelessly in tempo above the creekbank. His shot spun the helmet like a rock striking an empty bucket. No return fire; he climbed down to check his kill. The body on the riverbank was too small, in shorts and sandals: a darkhaired boy, the back of his head blown off. The helmet was gone, and there was no ocarina—maybe the stream took them. The urge to throw his rifle into the river and run was strong. But he resisted it: he took the accidental dead boy by one hand, and dragged him waist-deep, where the current took over. Then he returned to his tree.

The man is an expert of sorts, he hasn't survived the last forty years without knowing what's meant by a breaking twig, a swirl in the water fifty feet away. Varnished antlers and smallmouth bass and alligator jawbones on the walls testify to his knowledge. He doesn't have to rise from the sofa to see that across the river the boy is stumbling toward a bad end.

HURT TO SEE

A slight, unsteady hammering is all the street can bear this morning. A little boy's hammer, both claws missing. Neighbor children are driven to Sunday school; his parents prefer sleeping late. Sparrows bathe in the white dust of a depression in the oystershell driveway.

The boy hammers, he wonders how he'll come by a little sister. He asked for one. His mother stirred sugar into a pitcher of cooling tea. Maybe, she said, but she forgot to smile when she said it. By one scuffed knee, the boy has piled creek rocks: each rock he brings home he cracks, because one rock or another will be purple inside, or diamond, sharp as the picture in his father's book of rocks.

Barefoot in the shallow creek with wet pocketfuls of rock, he saw a huge white stork stalking. Storks eat crawfish; they used to bring babies—not anymore. If babies come now, they come in an ambulance. Yesterday he was pulling the shell off a crawfish when his mother's voice hurried out of the upstairs window—as though it hurt to see what he did. Scared, he dropped the animal before looking up. The thin bedroom curtains shivered a little. He heard his father do what—a sneeze? a bad cough? It sounded like he was crying. But Father told him when crawfish got too big for their shells they crawled out of them, all soft and new. He just wanted to see if it was true.

The boy brushes the white dust out of his work space, picks another rock. He's hungry, but can keep this up until they yell *Breakfast!* Between his spraddled legs he's pounded the sidewalk the hardest. The concrete is so cracked and chipped he'll have to smooth rock dust over it to keep his father from seeing, getting mad, making that ugly noise again.

RAZORS

The boy slumps in the barber chair, his hair's too long for Easter. If this were a tire swing chained to the live oak's arm, if it swung out over the crumbling river-bluff.... Barbers go bald faster than anyone else, that's why they crop a kid's head so close. And on Easter, a mother can hear whispers about longhair boys ten pews behind her. So he's getting flattopped the way his brother liked to, the way mother likes remembering him, the halfback, the All-America.

Between the way the boy's pout feels, and the way the mirror makes it look wrong, stand the bottles of scalp cream and shave lotion that smell like his brother did before dates. After his last haircut, the boy's teacher—who wears turtlenecks every Monday to cover her hickeys—told him barbers wear white because they used to be surgeons.

Two chairs down the oldest barber—totally bald—sits in his own chair reading a girlie magazine. He owns the green suede box with six gold-plated straight razors whose blades are engraved with every day of the week but Sunday. Each morning at eight he shaves the mayor, at nine the bishop. That old chair, the boy's father whispered one Friday, is where decisions get made. The rest of the week the old man wraps ordinary citizens in his hot-towel turban and lather.

Electric scissors hum at the back of the boy's neck. Do they save the mayor's whiskers? Will his own hair get swept into that pile? He's stuck between a mother-weepy Palm Sunday and playing lead guitar for the Animals. Eyes shut against the scissor-hum, he swings out from the oak, over a river the color of honey. The guitar squeals, he lets go of the rope.

His folks bring him here to get straightened out but there's not much hope of that. When his barber commands him to look, he opens his eyes to glossy blond breasts staring out of the bald barber's magazine. Short back and sides, flattop, it's what they do to your head in the Marines. They did it to his brother. Only last summer he swung on the bicep of his Marine-bald brother, who stood grinning and oak-proud on the lawn. Last summer, which will always stand between the All-America halfback trophy and a mortared bunker at Khe San.

STEALING DIRT

Would-be lovers, teenagers blue-cheeked with acne, always end up over the cemetery wall where they're not allowed. On the lip of a bricked-over vault they wobble to grab goofer dust, because dirt from a grave can turn a girl's head. Goofer dust scattered on her doorstep can make her think of love—even if only her sandal scuffs it while she helps her aunt bring groceries from the car.

Certain parlors still sell Controlling Oil in vials, plastic bags of Come-to-Me Powder. The boys don't have that kind of money, tourist money: the dozen tens and twenties in a monogrammed gold clip, wads of cash coughed out of red leather purses for paintings of dead jazz stars or a round-trip ticket anywhere, New York, London. "This town is nothing but souvenir shops," gripes one boy, poking his toe through the tip of his tennis shoe.

The other picks at his cheek, stares into the river. "Souvenir," his father told him, "is French for memory. Now remember that," he joked, peeling carrots for stew. The boy wants the English girl his father once knew: wants that other river ancient with swans and heavy-headed willows, wants the girl's sing-song in the prow of the flatboat rented for this memory he's still inheriting.

She lived in a brick flat with a creaky gate and gooseberry garden, his father said, nanny to French children marooned in Oxford. Willow-light fills the boy's head, he wants to be the river she puts her hand into. Father met her in a pub, they got half-drunk on pink gin and stole a bicycle. Along the river-path they bumped, her perched on the handlebars, until the front tire blew.

Her hair whips around the boy's head. It's midsummer eve sixteen years ago, another country. Somehow he's twenty and prepared not only to kiss but to undress this girl, whose name is Moira, who lights two candles in the little room. She would speak French in candlelight, Father tells him, faster than he could understand; afterward, she might translate a little.

His father was no father then, just a boy who ran out of money, who had to fly home. Months later he married the boy's mother—who left a long time ago. *Dead to me* is Father's phrase for her. But to think of the English girl peeling carrots over a sink, graying, telling a daughter how well she once spoke French, telling about this American boy....

The boy feels the stolen dirt in his pocket. What he wishes, he knows, is wishing on death. In the dresser drawer he isn't supposed to open, nestled between the .32 caliber revolver and the packet of Trojans, there's a swan feather: when he touches it, he can see the girl's head—heavy with sleep—filling his hand. She's asleep; he's a man. And though she can't hear, he's whispering that he won't run out, won't run out of money this time.

FLEUR-DE-LYS

They used to meet on the grounds of the condemned state hospital, to talk and kiss and do other things. A gray hulk, on hot days the hospital still exhales the ghost of an odor—iodine, formaldehyde. He'd park his convertible by the south gate, slip through a break in the kudzu-smothered iron fence. She'd park by the service entrance, and pass through a breezeway littered with glass and shreds of windowscreen.

Some afternoons on her way to him she'd pause, to peer into the solarium: nausea-green walls, ceiling high as a church, a dozen scattered wooden wheelchairs, some tipped backward. She liked to imagine some glamour had been in there: tubercular girls in fur stoles, bankers taking rest cures, Red Cross nurses with trays of sugary tea.

One afternoon, after the hour in the grass, her lover took her into the hospital basement. Take a good smell, he said, leading her past piss-yellow baths, the leather gurneys with sweat-darkened wrist and ankle straps. He wanted her to admit that not everything in town revolved around the convulsive, masked-ball seasons of the rich. But her husband was moving up too quickly in the shipping business to ignore. And his mother would disinherit him fast as a drink of water over a divorcée. They continued to meet, but less and less.

A month later a cop caught him at his usual exit, still tucking in his shirt. Wrapped in his jacket was an ornate fleur-de-lys he'd just jerked off the fence. Got your driver's license? the cop grinned. Trespassing and theft—he bit his lip and handed over the wallet. The cop inspected each snapshot and business card; he whistled as he pulled out the unused condom foil. Go home now, he said.

Home was a relief: 4:00 p.m. smell of café au lait, his mother's baby-powdered cheeks, the narcotic chimes of the hall clock. A relief more complete and final than all the hurried, grass-stained kisses. The iron fleur-de-lys still lies under the driver's seat of his car. Occasionally, vacuuming the carpets, he thinks about dragging it out. But why? It's hot to the touch; he can't abide passing it from hand to hand until it cools. There's as little reason to throw it out as burn himself. It does no harm staying right where it is.

LACTARIUS INDIGO

You can't judge a woman by the man who's allowed himself to hook the heel of his eelskin boot between the rungs of her barstool. Or by the three empty shot glasses she's turned over and slides under her fingertips in an idle parody of the shell game. Nothing under any of them for him. Some things stay hidden even from the man whose cheek and fingers will keep traces of her blush a full day after she's left his bed. How she knelt, a girl beneath the garish ceramic plaque of St. Anne, to pray that her grandfather would stop drinking paregoric from the bag in his vest pocket. How she taught herself to forage for wild asparagus and tiger lily buds in a disheveled orphan's cemetery, laid out in the heyday of typhoid.

She still knows the spore colors of mushrooms that kill. Another certain delectable mushroom she finds in pine woods so dense the only light that penetrates is religious. Beneath her fingernail, it drips an indigo milk that turns aquamarine. For every ten words a man tosses at her, she knows which one is worth something. Even if she singles a man out—one night after so many, lifting his glass and cigarette the same way at the same table—there will remain still and quiet inside her a sunset-drenched balcony overlooking the Gulf. Not even a gull will cry out—as she accompanies the man to his car—to let him know that the door leading up to that balcony has always been locked.

THE RESTRAINTS

Even when she was very little her hunger was worth something: hunger taught her to dance, and her father noticed. When his thirst was deep enough he could charm any bartender into clearing the narrow bar for just one dance—see, a girl, and feet so tiny. The patrons would shout for a second dance when they saw how the drumbeat of her bare feet could start such a trembling among the bottles on shelves. By the third or fourth dance, the trembling reached the glasses in their hands: they threw coins and bills at her feet to make her stop. Then Father would let her climb down and be a little girl again, mumbling thanks in poor English for the chair and spoon and bowls of stew brought her by drunken bricklayers and stevedores.

Afterward, under the stars of whatever field they slept in, she'd dream the same dream: dancing in a dress with ruffles, polka dots. Some nights, still asleep, she'd rise and wander. Once she woke in the middle of a dirt road: an armadillo sniffed her, a train blew in the distance. Another time she woke on the porch of an old white couple. Her English was so poor they guessed she was deaf-mute. They bathed and fed her, aimed to adopt her. She was trying on a dress with blue dots in front of their radio full of Bing Crosby when her father knocked at the screen door. He made her choose between the dress and him. To protect his livelihood after that, he tied a rope from her ankle to his ankle at night. If she rose to leave, she fell.

It is many dances later, now, many dresses, many men later. The nurses who are otherwise kind tie her old-lady wrists down so she cannot rip out the IV again. Some nights her feet drum against the footboard, but weakly. When she can forget the restraints, she goes over memories step by step: the time she was caught dancing in a bar at age ten and jailed for three days. Emerging, she saw Father at the corner holding his hat, which meant he was ashamed of himself. Out of his jacket he drew the most beautiful loaf of of bread, which she ate before allowing him to kiss her. She remembers the night her stitched-up knee opened on stage in Chicago: with every spin she flung blood onto the front-row gowns and tuxedos. By then even her blood was famous.

But sometimes when she was ten, twelve, dancing in those bars, she would not stop. Not even after her father's guitar stopped. She made the coins at her feet tremble and spin, kicked the sweaty dollar bills back at the drinkers and shouters. Having the moment, that was having everything. When she closes her eyes now she knows who it is, tied to her on the narrow bed.

IN COUNTRY

The war is far away by now, a book left open on the porch swing. A blank page softly taps against a page filled with tiny names. The man beside it sleeps carelessly—arm thrown backward over the swing, head lolling against the hard top slat. Waking up will hurt. A hot breeze starts up, the pages turn, image after paralyzed image. The man's legs needle him like phantom limbs; katydids fire short bursts in the pines.

Coming to, he forgets which country it is, despite the wisteria's evidence. The questioning could resume even here. Why shouldn't they use his grandmother's porch? Why not get him to see the dew slicking moon-whitened rails and columns, to inhale the childhood pungence of wisteria and river, if that makes him yield the truth? The empty pint bottle he kicks in the struggle to right himself proves nothing: maybe the interrogator got up to get another full one.

The bottle, the porch, the ache in his neck are as untrustworthy as a heaven built of nothing but unviolated memories. The goldfish in Grandmother's backyard pool, the ones he fed when he was a boy—they would not feed the eight children of a Cambodian farmer for even one meal. But he has seen children, all ribs and sores, combing monsoon-swollen bomb craters for frogs and carp. And earlier today, at the city zoo's reconstructed swamp, he watched kindergartners giggle and toss popcorn to alligators. It made him thirsty, made him feel he had been sentenced to life in the wrong country. They could have shot him. Instead they weakened him with questions, made him thin and sick. Then released him. Then freed him to watch the children of two worlds deal with hunger.

He picks up the book. This is the only way history can be grasped: between thumb and forefinger. History is made of paper, numbered, finite, it can be flipped forward or backward between drinks. At last it will put him to sleep. Just now he's running after the little girl, naked and crying, who keeps trying to outrun her napalm burns on the dike between paddies. No, he's the plaid-shirted man who feels the revolver pressed into his temple: who winces and involuntarily starts counting off the time lapse between hammer-cock and trigger-pull.

BRICK DUST

Eighteen years in the brickyard is seventeen years too long to try starting over. The laid-off man kicks at the dust a little; his foreman swears at luck. Carefully into the laid-off man's chest pocket he slides the pink slip, as though it was a Sunday handkerchief, a diploma. The brickyard, all red dust and noise, is bordered by a ten-foot-high brick wall both their fathers helped raise; they finish this difficulty in a corner, behind a pallet of maroon suburban brick. The laid-off man heads out the gate. The first bench he passes is brick—what else?—and he sits down on it hard, but not because of the layoff. All those cemetery Sundays with his father, they block the way home.

It was cash work in the Depression: seal and whitewash a dead person's oven after the funeral. Cemetery brick was flame-orange, crumbly—you could break it over your knee like a charred stick. As they loaded the body in, mourners stared or wept or shouted at the ground. He sat on crushed oystershells, dipping ants into buckets of mortar, buckets of whitewash. When the mourners left, he climbed up on the vault roof—damp grass and maidenhair fern—and followed clouds blowing in off the Gulf. His father worked the trowel tip around the mouth of the oven below: a patient, chipping sound.

He learned brick by helping lay out a wall of sixty rental ovens, fifteen across, four courses high, during one of the old man's layoffs. He even got a girl to crawl into one with him one night. He gave her a dollar, she undressed on the grass before climbing up. When he got home his underwear was pink with brick dust. The past is easy, it's a laugh. What's hard is what he can't do now. They don't rent brick ovens in the wall anymore; they plant the dead in the ground like everywhere else in the country.

What now? Cross the lawn on his knees, digging up dandelion roots. Patch the roof over the bathroom, work on the transmission of his neighbor's old Dodge. Meet his wife at the bus stop. Sit in the park—unemployment check in his pocket—watching families circle small columns of smoke from the brick barbecue pits. Watch them lean and dip into picnic bowls in a kind of folk dance. All over town he'll see things made of bricks he made, his father made. Eighteen years: he can't even afford a brick house.

And he'll still have to pass the brickyard to pick up bread and milk. Look up over the wall at the red dust, noisy and fine. Rising and settling, it can close a man up, choke him. It's still in his pores, the corners of his eyes. Can't scrub or cry it out, no matter how many years. His father died coughing it up, the red clay mucus the Bible called *Adam*.

GHOST POWDER

Neighbors left the peeling Victorian pile alone because it emitted sounds of cat hunger. But no one saw any cat sun itself on the viny porch railing or in a heavily curtained casement. And the old ghost-woman emerged only on trash pick-up days. Stepping around holes in the wraparound porch, she might pause on a step to check her face—china-doll white—in a scrap of hand mirror. Sometimes she tugged a nickel revolver out of her coat pocket, to see if it was still loaded. But she depended on white powder—patted into every bit of exposed face and neck and hands—to protect her hours of curbside rummaging. To a dressmaker, whose old dummy she loaded into a rusty shopping cart, she confided that white powder scared off drunks and black people. Her coat had been fashionable and black once, the dressmaker noticed. Now it was so powder-dusted it had turned ashen.

That winter there was a month of freezes, during which no one saw her scavenging. The paper plates of cornbread and boiled vegetables a nearby widow had been leaving at the door remained there for days. The beat policeman finally agreed to break in through a kitchen window early one evening. When the ambulance came, its red lights caromed among darkening rooms where neighbors sat trying to make children finish their dinners.

In his report, turned in late that night, the policeman chose to cite six things:

- the pervasion of cat urine and debris, including numerous small skeletons and mummies;
- the trash piled chest-high throughout the rooms, on chairs and tables and beds, mostly made up of old calendars, romance novels, and scraps of wire and metal;
- the dressmaker's dummy, which lay on an adjoining bed, partly dressed in a white evening jacket and cummerbund, with a sort of face and hair crayoned onto the wooden head;

- the pistol on the nightstand;
- the red streaks running up her legs, which had as their source several cat-scratches on her ankles and feet;
- the ten-pound bags of flour that lay on the vanity and bedroom floor, some apparently employed as cat litter, some scooped out, scattered, unaccounted for.

Privately he wondered how she could have survived on raw flour, without heat, electricity, running water. But conclusions were routinely left to his superiors. The loss of a leg to gangrene, or at least a foot, would be punishment enough for her, he guessed, let alone eviction and confinement. She had touched her pistol once, lightly, and asked him to go. He thought she ought to want to live. As for himself, he had a good deal of sick time built up; he planned to take it as soon as he could.

THE HAMMOCK PRAYER

Lately her legs are stiff, too stiff for her to get down on her knees behind the boy's chair. But it's the one place where he can't see how weak praying makes her. Cicadas have quit their loud day-long sawing, they creak like a rope hammock in the chinaberry-shaded evening cool. It's the time she used to unplug the iron and kneel, palm pressed to the back of the chair. More strength, she thought, flowed to his spine that way. Now she has to pray sitting across from his bamboo-thin legs. To his face she pretends it's sleep she's looking for, not God. But mid-prayer she'll squint: she won't stand for a fly walking near his open eye.

The doctor looked at her blood last week, said, Either quit taking in laundry or give the boy back to the city. The city gave her this boy too late for her knees to do him much good. He's the lightest-skinned child she's ever kept. And blue-eyed. In the quilted rocker stuffed with Spanish moss and with the white men's hair her husband swept up in his barbershop, nothing moves but those eyes. The blue so wide she believes it must hold something big—something flying past all he can't say or move to show her. When he naps, the eyes close; his mouth twists back into the chair's quilting, as though to suck its crackly, dry-moss center.

The first year she had the boy she could wheel him along the lakefront under river oaks. Fallen moss lay on the sand: she wove a handful into a beard, and set it on his cheeks. To see him as an old man tickled her, then hurt—neither of them had that long. She put the moss beard on herself to show how laughable it was. But in his eyes the thing kept flying: way past laughter, she thought, or else never to get there. Either way she was with him.

Then her husband's blood turned watery. He got too dizzy and falling-down to rise from that very chair. It still dizzies her to think some of the swept-up hair stuffed underneath the boy's legs may have come from his real father's head. So many motherless, fatherless children she bathed and fed and sent north: what did she get back? Postcards. Five minutes of long-distance static on holidays.

But this last boy, his eyes are wide enough to hold everything she's tried to do. She'd like to be strong enough to lift him into a hammock that creaks like cicada-song, strung between two riverside oaks. It would have to be a little river—no doctors, no social workers, no bleach-headed women demanding more starch. She'd lay him in the soft rope web and set it swinging. Maybe sit down against the tree herself, let the river lull her, the rope-creak. But she wouldn't doze off without seeing a butterfly light on his hand, crawling from knuckle to knuckle. She wouldn't sleep until she saw the butterfly show God where to begin.

THE ARCHWAY

Before he got too fat to get up from bed, he got stoned each morning and posed under the statue of Garibaldi. There he made foreigners pay to photograph his red hair: the braid so long he could flick a fly off his outstretched palm. Through his twenties he held street court beneath the liberator: small dope deals, odds on big games, when to slap a girl, how hard. One winter he caught a cold and started to swell from the ankles up. The dropsy had taken his father and brother, stretched them into huge infected water-skins. Now he grew too heavy to walk. Neighbors folded up the mattress around him, taxied him to Penn Station and bought him a berth on the train going south, where his brother had gone to die six years earlier.

The brother's widow has not forgotten how to make a man dying of his own weight still feel a little alive. His mounded water-weight spreads across a waterbed, over which she has hung a tiny remote-control TV. At the end of his right hand's reach glows a radio-alarm clock; at his left, the light dimmer and a thermos of lukewarm broth. But he has already tired of the daily fake excitement of game show contestants, fake struggles of wrestlers and evangelists. He has begun rebuilding the Washington Square arch, stone by stone, in his brain.

Over the past month he's mastered the dozen ranks of slabs in each pillar rising to the ledge of linked swastikas; the scabbards crossed over bundled arrows, supporting medallions crammed with heraldic shields; then the X of marching flags whose stone drapery is knotted underneath blank, bay-wreathed globes. On the arch, one angel blows a trumpet to the west; the other proffers an olive wreath to the east. The angels are separated by the keystone scroll with its confusion of fish-scales, upholstery buttons, fleur-de-lys, and one thick star. Over the star the eagle spreads its winged mantle, pigeonstained, slightly furled.

He has gotten so high on the arch that he feels himself lying beneath it, obstructed by pretzel carts, pigeon-flight, foreigners with fancy cameras. He strains to ignore them, and reconstruct what's inscribed above the multiple W's twined in oak and bay. The eave juts too far and he can't seem to slide back the imaginary distance that would make everything clear—*LET US RAISE A STANDARD TO WHICH THE WISE* is all he can read. His sister-in-law has offered to phone his ex-neighbors or look up the motto in a book. No, this task is his.

Each evening the broth gets a little colder before he tastes it. He's not going to allow one pigeon to alight on his arch until he can get past that huge noun *WISE,* until he can repair the rest of the words he used to live beneath. He frees his long oily braid from under the pillow where it usually lies coiled, and slaps its red tip against his free palm. Once again he goes over the rules of memory: No lovers will be allowed to lean against the base of his monument, no winos piss on it in the summer dark. And no mustard-slathered pretzels will get sold to the cops. More than once they hassled him: spread his legs with nightsticks, then shoved him through the archway toward their cruiser while he laughed and cursed, a faint stale fume of dope smoke and sweat shaken out of his clothes and hair toward Fifth Avenue, invisible, vanishing up in the exhaust of fat yellow taxis.

YELLOW STARS

A bashed air conditioner in the gutter stands for winter. Hundreds of spruces and pines—tightly bound, none taller than a man—are tossed out of dockside boxcars onto pallets, onto flatbed trucks. In delta spring, white dogwood petals advertised the five wounds of Jesus; the blood of Judas bloomed in the redbud. Now bare dogwoods and redbuds in the square blink on, off—pink, yellow, green.

On the avenue, three feet above everyone's head, bullhorns emit a stream of narcotized harmonies about snow, about chestnuts roasting. It's 64 degrees, overcast. If angels appeared now, they'd be put on a float. They'd be instructed to wave and grin at every runny-nosed child on the sidewalk.

A block east, two floors up, an old man has quit eating. Not for the night, not for Sunday to rest his gut—he's done with it. His daughter was run over by the Elysian Fields bus six months ago; he's too old to walk farther than the toilet. The son-in-law—a stevedore—can drink but can't cook. Tired from offloading dying evergreens since dawn, he brings home cold biscuits, white boxes of red beans and rice, half-eaten, congealed in pork fat. The old man finds them on the toilet seat. He dumps them in, and doesn't flush.

He's told himself this is a hunger strike. The radio was talking about prisoners in Ireland—that got him started. Mostly the radio tells him nothing he doesn't already know about weather, used cars, and presidents. At least it talks to him. It amuses him faintly: to be surrounded by a million people with radios who know about the different hungers in Ireland and Ethiopia, but don't know there's a hunger striker on Decatur Street.

Outside the locked bedroom door the son-in-law swears to himself again about the bus. Three more beers and he'll start in on the shittiness of stupid old bastards. The old man's bed is close enough to the window for him to monitor the fruit market across the street. A few days ago, in the first pangs of not eating, it was almost unbearable to watch the pyramid of navel oranges casually dismantled by hungry strangers, then rebuilt by the fruit-man. Now the glowing yellows, reds, and oranges of piled fruit interest him less than the image of his daughter at the stove. He remembers the care she took in breading his slices of okra and green tomato. It wasn't his lameness but his love of onions that made her weep.

He won't even have to think of her much longer. Let the cold come south, he says, and opens his window. Already the fruit-man has set out his first dozen lean Christmas trees against his crumbly brick wall. From one to the next he goes, affixing yellow poster-paper stars. Then, on each star, he scrawls the cost.

❦ The Author

Robert Hill Long, raised and educated in North Carolina, is the author of two previous books: *The Power to Die* and *The Work of the Bow,* both published by the Cleveland State University Poetry Center. His poems, prose poems, and flash fictions have appeared in anthologies including *Best American Poetry 1995* (Touchstone) and *Flash Fiction* (Norton), and in *Hudson Review, The Iowa Review, Kenyon Review, New England Review, Poetry, The Prose Poem, Virginia Quarterly Review, ZYZZYVA,* and many other magazines, as well as on the World Wide Web. He lives and works in Oregon.